LE COOKIE

cookies • whoopie pies
macarons • brownies • cupcakes

LE COOKIE

*Delicious sweet treats
designed in Paris,
baked in New York*

LONDON • NEW YORK

DESIGN, PHOTOGRAPHY AND PROP STYLING Steve Painter
COMMISSIONING EDITOR
Céline Hughes
HEAD OF PRODUCTION
Patricia Harrington
ART DIRECTOR Leslie Harrington
EDITORIAL DIRECTOR Julia Charles

INDEXER Hilary Bird
FOOD STYLING Lucy McKelvie
FOOD STYLIST'S ASSISTANT
Ellie Jarvis

First published in 2013 by
Ryland Peters & Small
20–21 Jockey's Fields
London WC1R 4BW
and
519 Broadway, 5th Floor
New York, NY 10012
www.rylandpeters.com

10 9 8 7 6 5 4 3 2 1

Printed in China

ISBN: 978-1-84975-346-3

A CIP record for this book is available from the British Library.

A CIP record for this book is available from the Library of Congress.

NOTES
• All spoon measurements are level unless otherwise specified.
• All butter is unsalted unless otherwise specified.
• All eggs are medium, unless otherwise specified. Recipes containing raw or partially cooked egg should not be served to the very young, very old, anyone with a compromised immune system or pregnant women.
• Ovens should be preheated to the specified temperatures. All ovens work slightly differently. We recommend using an oven thermometer and suggest you consult the maker's handbook for any special instructions, particularly if you are cooking in a fan-assisted/convection oven, as you will need to adjust temperatures according to manufacturer's instructions.

AUTHOR'S ACKNOWLEDGMENTS
This book would not have been possible without Benoit, the pastry chef and friend that changed my life, and of course my Sarah, who has already changed my future. Thank you so much for your support, friendship and love. And as it is my very first book to be published, I would like to hail my parents: thank you Mom and Dad for being here, always.

I would like also to thank my publisher Ryland Peters & Small, especially Céline and Julia for their commitment and professionalism, Steve for his beautiful photography and design, and Lucy for her wonderful food styling.

To all the readers, one word: enjoy!

CONTENTS

BIENVENUE A MOON STREET

Moon Street Pâtisserie is the brainchild of Mickael Benichou and Benoit Castel. Purveyor of luxury cookies, its aim is to give traditional gourmet American recipes a sophisticated French touch. Mickael had the idea back in 2010 of applying haute cuisine and innovation to established cookie recipes and collaborated with Benoit, an exceptional French pastry chef, to bring his idea to fruition.

With Benoit's experience in world renowned restaurants in Paris, and Mickael's talent for eye-catching design, Moon Street is a unique collaboration and now, with this book, you too can enter the glamorous world of Moon Street treats!

Cookies, brownies, whoopie pies, cupcakes or French macarons – whatever your preference, there's a cute and mouthwatering idea in these pages to inspire and surprise you. There are traditional chocolate chip cookies with a hint of orange, white chocolate brownies with an olive-oil twist, classic chocolate whoopies with French-inspired salted caramel, all-American cupcakes with a delightful lemon basil cream, and ultra-French macarons flavoured with cheesecake.

Allez! Jump in and see what you can create with these chic recipes for little morsels of deliciousness.

COOKIES

LE COOKIE

Le Cookie is the original and most traditional of our cookie recipes. Made with the best chocolate chips, freshest walnuts and purest vanilla extract you can buy, the ingredients will really shine. It seemed impossible to create a brand of cookies without starting with a classic, so this is Le Cookie, pure and simple!

100 g/7 tablespoons butter, at room temperature and chopped

80 g/7 tablespoons (caster) sugar

35 g/3 tablespoons muscovado or soft brown sugar

1 teaspoon pure vanilla extract

1 teaspoon single/light cream

1 egg

160 g/scant 1¼ cups plain/all-purpose flour

½ teaspoon baking powder

¼ teaspoon salt

135 g/¾ cup dark/semi-sweet chocolate chips

55 g/⅓ cup walnuts, chopped

1–2 baking sheets, lined with parchment paper

MAKES ABOUT 25

Put the butter in a bowl and beat with a wooden spoon until very soft. Beat in the sugars until well incorporated and creamy, then add the vanilla extract, cream and egg and beat in. Gradually sift in the flour, baking powder and salt and mix until combined. Finally, mix in the chocolate chips and walnuts.

Cover and refrigerate for 30 minutes.

Preheat the oven to 170°C (325°F) Gas 3.

Remove the bowl from the fridge. Lightly flour a clean work surface and roll the chilled dough out into a sausage roughly 30 cm/12 inches long. Cut the dough into about 25 equal slices and arrange on the prepared baking sheets.

Bake in the preheated oven for about 15–20 minutes until golden brown. Allow the cookies to cool on the baking sheets for 5 minutes, then transfer to a wire rack to finish cooling.

ORANGE CRUSH COOKIES

This may look like a classic chocolate chip cookie but take a bite and your taste buds will get a real treat. With orange extract and orange zest, this recipe is irresistible. Orange and dark/semi-sweet chocolate are a match made in heaven and work magically in a cookie.

120 g/1 stick butter, at room temperature and chopped

100 g/½ cup (caster) sugar

40 g/3½ tablespoons muscovado or soft brown sugar

2 teaspoons pure vanilla extract

1 drop of orange extract or orange flower water

2 teaspoons single/light cream

1 egg

180 g/1⅓ cups plain/all-purpose flour

1 teaspoon cocoa powder

½ teaspoon baking powder

¼ teaspoon salt

85 g/½ cup dark/semi-sweet chocolate chips

finely grated zest of ½ orange

1–2 baking sheets, lined with parchment paper

MAKES ABOUT 25

Put the butter in a bowl and beat with a wooden spoon until very soft. Beat in the sugars until well incorporated and creamy, then add the vanilla extract, orange extract or flower water, cream and egg and beat in. Gradually sift in the flour, cocoa powder, baking powder and salt and mix until combined. Finally, mix in the chocolate chips and orange zest.

Cover and refrigerate for 30 minutes.

Preheat the oven to 170°C (325°F) Gas 3.

Remove the bowl from the fridge. Lightly flour a clean work surface and roll the chilled dough out into a sausage roughly 30 cm/12 inches long. Cut the dough into about 25 equal slices and arrange on the prepared baking sheets.

Bake in the preheated oven for about 15–20 minutes until browned. Allow the cookies to cool on the baking sheets for 5 minutes, then transfer to a wire rack to finish cooling.

PRALINE CHIC COOKIES

Our Praline Chic cookie is the epitome of Parisian elegance. Delicate and sophisticated, it marries creamy milk chocolate with decadent praline for a truly refined treat.

110 g/1 stick butter, at room temperature and chopped

90 g/½ cup (caster) sugar

40 g/3½ tablespoons muscovado or soft brown sugar

1 teaspoon pure vanilla extract

1 teaspoon single/light cream

1 egg

190 g/1½ cups plain/all-purpose flour

½ teaspoon baking powder

¼ teaspoon salt

90 g/½ cup milk chocolate chips

40 g/2½ tablespoons almond praline paste (if you can't find it, use chocolate hazelnut paste)

1–2 baking sheets, lined with parchment paper

MAKES ABOUT 25

Put the butter in a bowl and beat with a wooden spoon until very soft. Beat in the sugars until well incorporated and creamy, then add the vanilla extract, cream and egg and beat in. Gradually sift in the flour, baking powder and salt and mix until combined. Finally, mix in the chocolate chips and almond praline paste.

Cover and refrigerate for 30 minutes.

Preheat the oven to 170°C (325°F) Gas 3.

Remove the bowl from the fridge. Lightly flour a clean work surface and roll the chilled dough out into a sausage roughly 30 cm/12 inches long. Cut the dough into about 25 equal slices and arrange on the prepared baking sheets.

Bake in the preheated oven for about 15–20 minutes until golden brown. Allow the cookies to cool on the baking sheets for 5 minutes, then transfer to a wire rack to finish cooling.

TRES YUMMY COOKIES

This is our limited edition cookie especially for the Christmas season – and for the true gourmet! It is a treasure trove of decadent flavours, with cocoa nibs and candied chestnut. Share a batch of these with family and friends if you can, or selfishly on your own if you can't…

100 g/7 tablespoons butter, at room temperature and chopped

80 g/7 tablespoons (caster) sugar

35 g/3 tablespoons muscovado or soft brown sugar

1 teaspoon pure vanilla extract

1 teaspoon single/light cream

1 egg

100 g/¾ cup plain/all-purpose flour

60 g/scant ½ cup chestnut flour

½ teaspoon baking powder

¼ teaspoon salt

85 g/½ cup milk chocolate chips

55 g/⅓ cup cocoa nibs

50 g/2 oz. candied chestnuts, chopped

1–2 baking sheets, lined with parchment paper

MAKES ABOUT 25

Put the butter in a bowl and beat with a wooden spoon until very soft. Beat in the sugars until well incorporated and creamy, then add the vanilla extract, cream and egg and beat in. Gradually sift in the flours, baking powder and salt and mix until combined. Finally, mix in the chocolate chips, cocoa nibs and candied chestnuts until evenly distributed.

Cover and refrigerate for 30 minutes.

Preheat the oven to 170°C (325°F) Gas 3.

Remove the bowl from the fridge. Lightly flour a clean work surface and roll the chilled dough out into a sausage roughly 30 cm/12 inches long. Cut the dough into about 25 equal slices and arrange on the prepared baking sheets.

Bake in the preheated oven for about 15–20 minutes until golden brown. Allow the cookies to cool on the baking sheets for 5 minutes, then transfer to a wire rack to finish cooling.

REBEL ROSE COOKIES

This is our signature cookie, and one with an innocent exterior that belies the rebellious rocker inside. Expect a rock 'n' roll combination of white chocolate and crystallized rose petals.

125 g/9 tablespoons butter, at room temperature and chopped

90 g/½ cup (caster) sugar

35 g/3 tablespoons muscovado or soft brown sugar

1 teaspoon pure vanilla extract

2 drops of rose extract (or a few drops of rose water)

2 teaspoons single/light cream

1 egg

200 g/1½ cups plain/all-purpose flour

½ teaspoon baking powder

½ teaspoon salt

90 g/½ cup white chocolate chips

15 g/½ oz. crystallized/candied rose petals, finely chopped

1 teaspoon crushed freeze-dried strawberries (optional)

1–2 baking sheets, lined with parchment paper

MAKES ABOUT 25

Put the butter in a bowl and beat with a wooden spoon until very soft. Beat in the sugars until well incorporated and creamy, then add the vanilla extract, rose extract or rose water, cream and egg and beat in. Gradually sift in the flour, baking powder and salt and mix until combined. Finally, mix in the chocolate chips, rose petals and freeze-dried strawberries, if using.

Cover and refrigerate for 30 minutes.

Preheat the oven to 170°C (325°F) Gas 3.

Remove the bowl from the fridge. Lightly flour a clean work surface and roll the chilled dough out into a sausage roughly 30 cm/12 inches long. Cut the dough into about 25 equal slices and arrange on the prepared baking sheets.

Bake in the preheated oven for about 15–20 minutes until golden brown. Allow the cookies to cool on the baking sheets for 5 minutes, then transfer to a wire rack to finish cooling.

BROWNIES

BONJOUR BROWNIES

This is a classic and delicious recipe with macadamias and walnuts to get you into the brownie spirit. It is very important to cream the butter well, as it will add softness to the brownie while the nuts add some excellent crunch.

240 g/8½ oz. dark/bittersweet chocolate (55% cocoa), chopped

100 g/7 tablespoons butter, at room temperature and chopped

120 g/generous ½ cup (caster) sugar

2 eggs

60 ml/¼ cup semi-skimmed milk

120 g/1 scant cup plain/all-purpose flour

25 g/¼ cup ground almonds

1 teaspoon baking powder

1 vanilla bean

20 g/2 tablespoons macadamia nuts

20 g/2 tablespoons walnuts, chopped

20-cm/8-inch square baking pan, greased and dusted with flour

MAKES 6–8

Preheat the oven to 190°C (375°F) Gas 5.

Put the chocolate in a heatproof bowl set over a saucepan of barely simmering water. Do not let the base of the bowl touch the water. Allow to melt, stirring occasionally, until completely smooth. Remove from the heat.

Put the butter in a bowl and beat with a wooden spoon until very soft. Beat in the sugar until well incorporated, then beat in one egg at a time. Add the milk and stir in. Add the flour, almonds and baking powder and beat in. Split the vanilla bean lengthways and scrape the seeds out into the bowl. Pour the melted chocolate in too and mix everything together well. Finally, stir in the macadamias and walnuts.

Spoon the mixture into the prepared baking pan, spread level with a spatula and bake in the preheated oven for about 20 minutes. Allow the brownies to cool in the pan for a few minutes, then turn out onto a wire rack to cool completely.

Serve at room temperature, cut into equal portions.

SUGAR AND SPICE BROWNIES

Aromatic cardamom and milk chocolate are a match made in brownie heaven – try it and love it!

100 g/3½ oz. milk chocolate, chopped

200 g/1 stick plus 6 tablespoons butter, chopped

3 pinches of ground cardamom

3 eggs

190 g/1 scant cup (caster) sugar

100 g/¾ cup plain/ all-purpose flour

40 g/⅓ cup glacé/candied cherries, chopped

20-cm/8-inch square baking pan, greased and dusted with flour

MAKES 6-8

Preheat the oven to 170°C (325°F) Gas 3.

Put the chocolate and butter in a heatproof bowl set over a saucepan of barely simmering water. Do not let the base of the bowl touch the water. Allow to melt, stirring occasionally, until completely smooth. Add the cardamom and stir in with a wooden spoon. Remove from the heat.

In a separate bowl, whisk the eggs and sugar for 1–2 minutes. Sift in the flour and whisk again to mix. Pour the chocolate mixture in and mix well with the wooden spoon. Finally, stir in the cherries.

Spoon the mixture into the prepared baking pan, spread level with a spatula and bake in the preheated oven for about 25 minutes. Allow the brownies to cool in the pan for a few minutes, then turn out onto a wire rack to cool completely.

Serve at room temperature, cut into equal portions.

THE SUPREME

This is a dessert our chef created when he was working with the renowned Hélène Darroze at her restaurant. The Baileys syrup adds a caramel sweetness offset by the orange and lemon zest, cinnamon and nutmeg. Pouring the syrup over the brownie will allow it to seep in and turn it into more of a sticky dessert.

225 g/8 oz. dark/bittersweet chocolate (55% cocoa), chopped

200 g/1 stick plus 6 tablespoons butter, chopped

4 eggs

130 g/⅔ cup (caster) sugar

125 g/1 scant cup plain/all-purpose flour

BAILEYS SYRUP

1 vanilla bean

finely grated zest of ½ orange

finely grated zest of ½ lemon

¼ teaspoon ground cinnamon

¼ teaspoon ground nutmeg

50 g/¼ cup (caster) sugar

50 ml/¼ cup Baileys Irish Cream liqueur

20-cm/8-inch square baking pan, greased and dusted with flour

MAKES 6–8

Preheat the oven to 170°C (325°F) Gas 3.

Put the chocolate and butter in a heatproof bowl set over a saucepan of barely simmering water. Do not let the base of the bowl touch the water. Allow to melt, stirring occasionally, until completely smooth. Remove from the heat.

In a separate bowl, whisk the eggs and sugar for 1–2 minutes. Sift in the flour and whisk again to mix. Pour the chocolate mixture in and mix well with a wooden spoon.

Spoon the mixture into the prepared baking pan, spread level with a spatula and bake in the preheated oven for about 25 minutes. Remove from the oven and leave in the baking pan while you make the Baileys syrup.

To make the Baileys syrup, split the vanilla bean lengthways and scrape the seeds out into a small saucepan. Add the citrus zest, cinnamon, nutmeg, sugar and 50 ml/¼ cup cold water and gently bring to the boil. Stir in the Baileys.

Brush the syrup evenly over the warm brownie in the pan, using a pastry brush, then allow to cool.

Serve at room temperature, cut into equal portions.

COFFEE LOVER'S BROWNIES

Chocolate and coffee make for a heavenly after-dinner treat. In this simple recipe, the coffee enhances the taste of the chocolate and gives the brownie a sophisticated depth of flavour.

225 g/8 oz. dark/bittersweet chocolate (55% cocoa), chopped

200 g/1 stick plus 6 tablespoons butter, chopped

4 eggs

130 g/⅔ cup (caster) sugar

125 g/1 scant cup plain/ all-purpose flour

1½ tablespoons instant coffee or espresso granules

20-cm/8-inch square baking pan, greased and dusted with flour

MAKES 6-8

Preheat the oven to 170°C (325°F) Gas 3.

Put the chocolate and butter in a heatproof bowl set over a saucepan of barely simmering water. Do not let the base of the bowl touch the water. Allow to melt, stirring occasionally, until completely smooth. Remove from the heat.

In a separate bowl, whisk the eggs and sugar for 1–2 minutes. Sift in the flour, add the coffee and whisk again to mix. Pour the chocolate mixture in and mix well with a wooden spoon.

Spoon the mixture into the prepared baking pan, spread level with a spatula and bake in the preheated oven for about 25 minutes. Allow the brownies to cool in the pan for a few minutes, then turn out onto a wire rack to cool completely.

Serve at room temperature, cut into equal portions.

BIJOUX BLONDIES

This unusual recipe was inspired by a dessert our chef tried in Spain. Using extra virgin olive oil in the brownie mixture renders a rich, deliciously tender texture. Use the finest quality white chocolate you can find with as little sugar as possible for the best result.

250 g/9 oz. white chocolate, chopped

120 g/1 stick butter, chopped

½ tablespoon sweet extra virgin olive oil

4 eggs

140 g/¾ cup (caster) sugar

90 g/⅔ cup plain/all-purpose flour

70 g/½ cup blanched almonds, chopped

WHITE CHOCOLATE AND OLIVE OIL GANACHE

1 vanilla bean

90 ml/⅓ cup single/light cream

180 g/6½ oz. white chocolate, chopped

40 ml/3 tablespoons sweet extra virgin olive oil

blanched almonds, to decorate

20-cm/8-inch square baking pan, greased and dusted with flour

MAKES 6–8

Preheat the oven to 170°C (325°F) Gas 3.

Put the white chocolate and butter in a heatproof bowl set over a saucepan of barely simmering water. Do not let the base of the bowl touch the water. Allow to melt, stirring occasionally, until completely smooth. Stir in the olive oil. Remove from the heat.

In a separate bowl, whisk the eggs and sugar for 1–2 minutes. Sift in the flour and whisk again to mix. Pour the chocolate mixture in and mix well with a wooden spoon. Finally, stir in the chopped almonds.

Spoon the mixture into the prepared baking pan, spread level with a spatula and bake in the preheated oven for about 20 minutes. Allow to cool completely in the pan.

To make the white chocolate and olive oil ganache, split the vanilla bean lengthways and scrape the seeds out into a saucepan. Add the cream and gently bring to the boil. Meanwhile, put the chocolate in a heatproof bowl set over a saucepan of barely simmering water. Do not let the base of the bowl touch the water. Allow to melt, stirring occasionally, until completely smooth. Add the olive oil and stir in. Remove from the heat and pour in the boiled cream. Beat with an electric whisk until smooth and glossy. Spread the ganache evenly over the cold brownie in the pan and refrigerate overnight.

When you are ready to serve, cut the brownie into equal portions and decorate each one with a blanched almond.

CRACKLING BROWNIE FRENCH FRIES

This clever idea has the wow factor and is perfect for surprising dinner guests! Popping candy adds crackle inside the brownie, then if you cut it into large French fries, you can dip them in chocolate hazelnut spread and finish with more popping candy. American brownies meet French fries – c'est cool!

240 g/8½ oz. dark/bittersweet chocolate (55% cocoa), chopped

100 g/7 tablespoons butter, at room temperature and chopped

120 g/⅔ cup (caster) sugar

2 eggs

60 ml/¼ cup semi-skimmed milk

120 g/1 scant cup plain/all-purpose flour

25 g/¼ cup ground almonds

1 teaspoon baking powder

1 vanilla bean

2 bags of popping candy, plus extra to serve

chocolate hazelnut spread, to serve

20-cm/8-inch square baking pan, greased and dusted with flour

MAKES 6–8

Preheat the oven to 190°C (375°F) Gas 5.

Put the chocolate in a heatproof bowl set over a saucepan of barely simmering water. Do not let the base of the bowl touch the water. Allow to melt, stirring occasionally, until completely smooth. Remove from the heat.

Put the butter in a bowl and beat with a wooden spoon until very soft. Beat in the sugar until well incorporated and creamy, then beat in one egg at a time. Add the milk and stir in. Add the flour, almonds and baking powder and beat in. Split the vanilla bean lengthways and scrape the seeds out into the bowl. Pour the melted chocolate in and add the popping candy. Mix everything together well.

Spoon the mixture into the prepared baking pan, spread level with a spatula and bake in the preheated oven for about 15–20 minutes. Allow to cool in the pan for a few minutes, then turn out onto a wire rack to cool completely.

Cut up the brownie into fat fries and serve with chocolate hazelnut spread for dipping in and extra popping candy for sprinkling over.

WHOOPIES

VERY BERRY WHOOPIES

This is a delicate interpretation of a traditional American whoopie pie – the ultimate bite-size 'sweet sandwich'. It would make a gorgeously luxurious picnic treat. It is also a lovely example of our mission to take classic, much-loved bakes and give them a modern or quirky twist with new flavours, techniques or presentation.

1 quantity Vanilla Whoopie Shells (page 34)

fresh berries, to fill (chopped if large)

VANILLA CHANTILLY

½ vanilla bean

250 ml/1 cup whipping cream

25 g/3 tablespoons icing/ confectioners' sugar, plus extra to dust

piping bag plus plain and star-shaped nozzles/tips

baking sheet, lined with non-stick parchment paper

MAKES ABOUT 15

Preheat the oven to 190˚C (375˚F) Gas 5.

Make and bake the Vanilla Whoopie Shells as described on page 34.

To make the vanilla chantilly, split the vanilla bean lengthways and scrape the seeds out into a bowl. Add the cream and sugar and beat with an electric whisk until it is firm enough to pipe.

Fit the piping bag with a star-shaped nozzle/tip and fill it with the chantilly. Pipe a small amount onto the flat underside of half of the cold whoopie pies. Add some berries and sandwich with another whoopie pie shell.

Dust with icing/confectioners' sugar just before serving.

MADE-IN-FRANCE WHOOPIES

In the Brittany region of France, 'caramel au beurre salé' – salted caramel – is a local specialty. Since our chef hails from this region, it made sense to create a whoopie recipe to remind him of home.

CHOCOLATE WHOOPIE SHELLS

6 eggs, separated

170 g/generous ¾ cup (caster) sugar

130 g/1 cup plain/all-purpose flour

40 g/scant ½ cup cocoa powder

SALTED CARAMEL CREAM

100 ml/⅓ cup plus 1 tablespoon single/light cream

100 g/3½ oz. chewy toffee sweets/candy, plus extra, chopped, to fill

25 g/2 tablespoons salted butter

200 g/7 oz. mascarpone

piping bag, fitted with a plain nozzleltip

baking sheet, lined with non-stick parchment paper

MAKES ABOUT 15

Preheat the oven to 190°C (375°F) Gas 5.

To make the chocolate whoopie shells, put the egg whites and sugar in a grease-free stainless-steel mixing bowl and whisk with an electric whisk until white and glossy and stiff peaks have formed. Lightly beat the egg yolks in a separate bowl to loosen them, then gently fold into the egg whites with a large metal spoon. Sift in the flour and cocoa powder and fold in until evenly incorporated.

Fill the piping bag with the mixture. Pipe about 30 large rounds of the mixture on the prepared baking sheet. Space the rounds roughly 6 cm/2½ inches apart. Alternatively, you can spoon the mixture neatly onto the baking sheet using 2 tablespoons.

Bake in the preheated oven for about 12 minutes. Remove from the oven and allow to cool on the baking sheet.

To make the salted caramel cream, pour the cream into a saucepan and gently bring to the boil. Add the toffee sweets/candy and cook over low–medium heat until all the toffees have melted. Now add the butter and stir until melted and smooth. Transfer to a bowl, allow to cool slightly, then refrigerate until cold.

Add the mascarpone to the chilled salted caramel and whisk with the electric whisk just until the caramel is evenly incorporated. Fill the piping bag with the salted caramel cream. Pipe a small amount onto the flat underside of half of the cold whoopie pies. Add some chopped toffees and sandwich with another whoopie pie shell.

FIT-FOR-A-QUEEN WHOOPIES

Our chef's numerous trips to London have inspired him to dream up a whoopie pie fit for a queen. Rich mascarpone cream flavoured with raspberry jam and studded with blueberries makes this batch of pretty pies a splendid centrepiece for a royal tea party.

icing/confectioners' sugar, to dust

VANILLA WHOOPIE SHELLS

½ vanilla bean

6 eggs, separated

150 g/¾ cup (caster) sugar

150 g/1 cup plus 2 tablespoons plain/all-purpose flour

FRUITY FILLING

150 g/½ cup raspberry jam

150 g/5½ oz. mascarpone

blueberries, to fill

piping bag, fitted with a plain nozzle/tip

baking sheet, lined with non-stick parchment paper

MAKES ABOUT 15

Preheat the oven to 190°C (375°F) Gas 5.

To make the vanilla whoopie shells, split the vanilla bean lengthways and scrape the seeds out into a grease-free stainless-steel mixing bowl. Add the egg whites and sugar and whisk with an electric whisk until white and glossy and stiff peaks have formed. Lightly beat the egg yolks in a separate bowl to loosen them, then gently fold into the egg whites with a large metal spoon. Sift in the flour and fold in until evenly incorporated.

Fill the piping bag with the mixture. Pipe about 30 large rounds of the mixture on the prepared baking sheet. Space the rounds roughly 6 cm/2½ inches apart. Alternatively, you can spoon the mixture neatly onto the baking sheet using 2 tablespoons.

Bake in the preheated oven for about 12 minutes. Remove the whoopies from the oven and allow to cool on the baking sheet.

To make the fruity filling, put the raspberry jam and mascarpone in a bowl and whisk with an electric whisk just until the jam is evenly incorporated. Fill the piping bag with the fruity filling. Pipe a small amount onto the flat underside of half of the cold whoopie pies. Add some blueberries and sandwich with another whoopie pie shell.

Dust with icing/confectioners' sugar just before serving.

WICKED PECAN PIE WHOOPIES

French-style pecan nougatine brings to mind crunchy, sticky American pecan pie, so what better way to celebrate this happy coincidence than in a wickedly indulgent pecan pie whoopie?

1 quantity Chocolate Whoopie Shells (page 33)

CHOCOLATE CREAM

100 ml/⅓ cup milk

100 ml/½ cup single/light cream

2 egg yolks

20 g/1½ tablespoons (caster) sugar

200 g/7 oz. dark/bittersweet chocolate (65% cocoa), chopped

PECAN NOUGATINE

pat of butter

40 g/⅓ cup pecans, chopped

100 g/½ cup (caster) sugar

piping bag, fitted with a plain nozzle/tip

baking sheet, lined with non-stick parchment paper

non-stick baking sheet

MAKES ABOUT 15

To make the chocolate cream, start the day before you want to bake the whoopies. Pour the milk and cream into a saucepan and gently bring to the boil. Meanwhile, put the egg yolks and sugar in a bowl and beat with an electric whisk until thick and pale, and the beaters leave a thick ribbon trail when you lift them out of the mixture. Transfer to the saucepan of milk/cream over very low heat. Heat until just below simmering point – when you dip a wooden spoon in and lift it out again, it should coat the back of the spoon. Add half the chocolate and stir until melted and smooth. Transfer to a bowl, cover and refrigerate for 24 hours.

The next day, preheat the oven to 190°C (375°F) Gas 5, and make and bake the Chocolate Whoopie Shells as described on page 33.

To make the pecan nougatine, melt the butter in a frying pan, then add the pecans and fry until nicely toasted. Put the sugar and 2½ tablespoons water in a small saucepan over medium heat and heat until the sugar has melted. Bring to the boil, then lower the heat and simmer for 2–3 minutes, stirring with a wooden spoon until caramelized. Stir in the toasted pecans. Pour onto the non-stick baking sheet and spread it with an oiled spatula. Allow to cool until set. When set, finely chop with a sharp knife.

Fill the piping bag with the chocolate cream. Pipe a small amount onto the flat underside of half of the cold whoopie pies. Add some chopped pecan nougatine (reserving a little for decorating) and sandwich with another whoopie pie shell.

Melt the remaining chocolate and allow to cool slightly. Carefully dip the whoopie pies into the chocolate and sprinkle with more chopped nougatine. Allow to set.

FIT-FOR-THE-KING WHOOPIES

I always loved banana split as a child and it was one of the first American desserts I ever tried, so we came up with this whoopie in its honour. But in fact it also bears all the hallmarks of Elvis' favourite snack – fried banana and peanut butter sandwiches – so we've named this after him.

1 quantity Chocolate Whoopie Shells (page 33)

3–4 ripe bananas, sliced, to fill

cocoa powder, to dust

PEANUT BUTTER CREAM

150 g/⅔ cup peanut butter (smooth or crunchy, as preferred)

150 g/5½ oz. mascarpone

piping bag, fitted with a plain nozzleltip

baking sheet, lined with non-stick parchment paper

MAKES ABOUT 15

Preheat the oven to 190°C (375°F) Gas 5.

Make and bake the Chocolate Whoopie Shells as described on page 33.

To make the peanut butter cream, put the peanut butter and mascarpone in a bowl and whisk with a balloon whisk or electric whisk until combined.

Fill the piping bag with the peanut butter cream. Pipe a small amount onto the flat underside of half of the cold whoopie pies. Add a few slices of banana and sandwich with another whoopie pie shell.

Dust with cocoa powder just before serving.

JELLO WHIPPED CREAM WHOOPIES

This is a special recipe to please so many people! No matter where you're from, you probably had jello whipped cream or jelly and cream as a child. You might even now be partial to an English trifle. Take the elements of these desserts, give them a French twist with grenadine syrup and chantilly cream, and this is what you get!

1 quantity Vanilla Whoopie Shells (page 34)

GRENADINE JELLY

3 gelatine leaves (or unflavoured gelatine powder used according to manufacturer's instructions)

40 g/3 tablespoons (caster) sugar

1 tablespoon grenadine syrup

red food colouring

VANILLA CHANTILLY

½ vanilla bean

250 ml/1 cup whipping cream

25 g/3 tablespoons icing/confectioners' sugar, plus extra to dust

piping bag plus plain and star-shaped nozzles/tips

baking sheet, lined with non-stick parchment paper

MAKES ABOUT 15

Preheat the oven to 190°C (375°F) Gas 5.

Make and bake the Vanilla Whoopie Shells as described on page 34.

To make the grenadine jelly, soak the gelatine leaves in a bowl of cold water to soften them. Meanwhile, put 100 ml/7 tablespoons water and the sugar into a saucepan and gently bring to the boil, making sure the sugar has dissolved. Remove from the heat, squeeze the excess water out of the gelatine leaves and add to the hot sugar syrup with the grenadine syrup and enough red food colouring to make your desired shade of red. Stir until the gelatine has completely dissolved. Pour into a container of the right size for the mixture to be no more than 1 cm/½ inch deep. Refrigerate for 2 hours to set.

To make the vanilla chantilly, split the vanilla bean lengthways and scrape the seeds out into a bowl. Add the cream and sugar and beat with an electric whisk until it is firm enough to pipe.

Fit the piping bag with a star-shaped nozzle/tip and fill it with the chantilly. Pipe a small amount onto the flat underside of half of the cold whoopie pies. Chop the set jelly into tiny cubes and arrange some on top of the chantilly. Sandwich with the remaining whoopie pie shells.

Dust with icing/confectioners' sugar just before serving.

CUPCAKES

GOOD-AS-GOLD CUPCAKES

Sometimes, simple is best. A chocolate-flecked vanilla base topped with airy chocolate cream and embellished with a precious, bejewelled finishing touch makes for a cupcake that's as good as gold.

1 quantity Vanilla Cupcake Mixture (page 46, but follow the method here)

45 g/⅓ cup chocolate vermicelli

gold leaf, chocolate chips and edible gold lustre dust, to decorate

CHOCOLATE CREAM

1 gelatine leaf (or unflavoured gelatine powder used according to manufacturer's instructions)

300 ml/1⅓ cups single/light cream

200 g/7 oz. milk chocolate, finely chopped

cupcake pan, lined with 12 cupcake cases

piping bag, fitted with a star-shaped nozzleltip

MAKES 12

To make the Vanilla Cupcake Mixture, start the day before you want to bake the cupcakes. Make the mixture as described on page 46 but fold the chocolate vermicelli in at the end. Cover and refrigerate for 24 hours.

The next day, preheat the oven to 160°C (325°F) Gas 3.

Divide the chilled mixture between the cupcake cases and bake in the preheated oven for about 15–20 minutes. Remove from the oven and allow to cool completely.

To make the chocolate cream, soak the gelatine leaf in a bowl of cold water to soften it. Meanwhile, pour the cream into a saucepan and gently bring to the boil. Remove from the heat, squeeze the excess water out of the gelatine leaf and add it to the hot cream, stirring until the gelatine has completely dissolved. Put the chopped chocolate in a heatproof bowl, pour the hot cream over it and stir until completely melted and smooth. Allow to cool slightly, then refrigerate until completely cold.

Remove the chocolate cream from the fridge and whisk with an electric whisk until smooth, unctuous and holding stiff peaks. Fill the piping bag with the chocolate cream and pipe it on top of the cold cupcakes. Decorate with gold leaf and chocolate chips and dust with edible gold lustre dust.

MON CHERRY AMOUR CUPCAKES

This has got to be the Valentine's Day cupcake, for both couples and sweet-toothed singletons. The Kirsch adds a hint of liquorice to the buttercream. What better way to celebrate your love of cupcakes?

1 quantity Vanilla Cupcake Mixture (page 46, but follow the method here)

50 g/½ cup finely chopped pistachios, plus extra to decorate

12 glacé/candied cherries

PISTACHIO BUTTERCREAM

180 g/1½ sticks butter, at room temperature

320 g/2¼ cups icing/confectioners' sugar

50 ml/3½ tablespoons milk

1 tablespoon pure vanilla extract

2 tablespoons pistachio paste*

1 tablespoon Kirsch cherry liqueur

green food colouring (optional)

cupcake pan, lined with 12 cupcake cases

piping bag, fitted with a star-shaped nozzle/tip

MAKES 12

To make the Vanilla Cupcake Mixture, start the day before you want to bake the cupcakes. Make the mixture as described on page 46 and fold in the chopped pistachios at the end. Cover and refrigerate for 24 hours.

The next day, preheat the oven to 160°C (325°F) Gas 3.

Divide the mixture between the cupcake cases and bake in the preheated oven for about 15–20 minutes. Remove from the oven and allow to cool completely.

To make the pistachio buttercream, put the butter, sugar, milk, vanilla extract, pistachio paste and Kirsch in a bowl and beat with an electric whisk or by hand with a wooden spoon until you get a light, fluffy texture. Stir in drops of the food colouring until you get the desired shade of pistachio green, if you like.

Fill the piping bag with the buttercream and pipe on top of the cold cupcakes. Balance a glacé/candied cherry on top and sprinkle extra chopped pistachios around the edge.

*To make your own pistachio paste, roast 125 g/1 cup pistachios on a baking sheet in a preheated oven at 160°C (325°F) Gas 3 for 10 minutes, taking care not to let them burn. Transfer to a bowl. Put 175 ml/⅔ cup water and 60 g/⅓ cup (caster) sugar in a saucepan and bring to the boil. When the sugar has dissolved and the liquid is boiling, cook over medium heat for 5 minutes. Carefully pour this syrup into a food processor with the roasted pistachios and 30 g/⅓ cup ground almonds and pulse until you get a smooth paste.

PAVLOVA CUPCAKES

The beloved pavlova dessert was invented to honour the Russian ballerina, Anna Pavlova. This cupcake rendition is an ode to her elegance and grace, and everyone who sets eyes on it will fall in love.

fresh raspberries, meringue chips, finely chopped freeze-dried raspberries and edible silver lustre dust, to decorate

VANILLA CUPCAKE MIXTURE

½ vanilla bean

3 eggs

150 g/1 cup icing/confectioners' sugar

150 g/1 cup plus 2 tablespoons plain/all-purpose flour

1 teaspoon baking powder

150 g/1 stick plus 3 tablespoons butter, melted

VANILLA CHANTILLY

1 vanilla bean

450 ml/1¾ cups whipping cream

45 g/5 tablespoons icing/confectioners' sugar

cupcake pan, lined with 12 cupcake cases

piping bag, fitted with a star-shaped nozzleltip

MAKES 12

To make the vanilla cupcake mixture, start the day before you want to bake the cupcakes. Split the vanilla bean lengthways and scrape the seeds out into a bowl. Add the eggs and sugar and beat with an electric whisk until tripled in volume and the beaters leave a thick ribbon trail when you lift them out of the mixture.

Sift the flour and baking powder into the bowl and whisk lightly. Add the melted butter and fold in gently with a large metal spoon. Cover and refrigerate for 24 hours.

The next day, preheat the oven to 160°C (325°F) Gas 3.

Divide the mixture between the cupcake cases and bake in the preheated oven for about 15–20 minutes. Remove from the oven and allow to cool completely.

To make the vanilla chantilly, split the vanilla bean lengthways and scrape the seeds out into a bowl. Add the cream and sugar and beat with an electric whisk until it is firm enough to pipe.

Fill the piping bag with the chantilly and pipe on top of the cold cupcakes. Decorate with fresh raspberries, meringue chips and freeze-dried raspberries and dust with edible silver lustre dust.

CUPCAKES DU JARDIN

As pretty as Paris in spring, this is the perfect cupcake to make when winter is vanishing, the days are getting longer and the sun is brightening up our lives. We decided to top our vanilla-lemon cupcake with a very light and summery lemon basil cream. Our chef loves adding a fresh and fruity taste to desserts!

1 quantity Vanilla Cupcake Mixture (page 46, but follow the method here)

grated zest of ½ lemon

wild strawberries and freshly chopped basil, to decorate

LEMON BASIL CREAM

220 g/¾ cup lemon jam (yes jam, not curd!)

5 fresh basil leaves

250 g/9 oz. mascarpone

cupcake pan, lined with 12 cupcake cases

piping bag, fitted with a star-shaped nozzleltip

MAKES 12

To make the Vanilla Cupcake Mixture, start the day before you want to bake the cupcakes. Make the mixture as described on page 46 and fold in the lemon zest at the end. Cover and refrigerate for 24 hours.

The next day, preheat the oven to 160°C (325°F) Gas 3.

Divide the mixture between the cupcake cases and bake in the preheated oven for about 15–20 minutes. Remove from the oven and allow to cool completely.

To make the lemon basil cream, put the lemon jam and basil leaves in a food processor and blitz until smooth. Fold this gently into the mascarpone until evenly mixed.

Fill the piping bag with the lemon basil cream and pipe on top of the cold cupcakes. Decorate with wild strawberries and chopped basil.

DULCE DE LECHE CUPCAKES

Dulce de leche has a butterscotch caramel flavour that goes really well with chocolate. It originates from South America but in France, we have something similar called 'confiture de lait' which is just as sticky, sweet and deliciously addictive. Adding ground almonds and milk chocolate chips to the base of these cupcakes gives them an interesting texture.

1 quantity Vanilla Cupcake Mixture (page 46, but follow the method here)

45 g/⅓ cup milk chocolate chips

30 g/⅓ cup ground almonds

DULCE DE LECHE CREAM

½ vanilla bean

230 g/⅔ cup dulce de leche, plus extra to drizzle

250 g/9 oz. mascarpone

cupcake pan, lined with 12 cupcake cases

piping bag, fitted with a star-shaped nozzle/tip

MAKES 12

To make the Vanilla Cupcake Mixture, start the day before you want to bake the cupcakes. Make the mixture as described on page 46 and fold in the chocolate chips and ground almonds at the end. Cover and refrigerate for 24 hours.

The next day, preheat the oven to 160°C (325°F) Gas 3.

Divide the mixture between the cupcake cases and bake in the preheated oven for about 15–20 minutes. Remove from the oven and allow to cool completely.

To make the dulce de leche cream, split the vanilla bean lengthways and scrape the seeds out into a bowl. Add the dulce de leche and mix with a balloon whisk or fork to loosen it, then fold in the mascarpone.

Fill the piping bag with the cream and pipe on top of the cold cupcakes. Drizzle dulce de leche on top.

MACARONS

FLOWER POWER MACARONS

This is a sophisticated macaron with a subtle and delicate mixture of flavours: rose, lychee, raspberry and white chocolate. For an extra-special touch, tint the ganache in different shades of pink using food colouring paste. Make a batch of these and you're guaranteed to want to eat them all in a single sitting!

1 quantity Vanilla Macaron Shells (page 60, but follow the method here)

finely chopped crystallized rose petals, to sprinkle

about 7 lychees, peeled, pitted and quartered, to fill

RASPBERRY GANACHE

400 g/14 oz. raspberry purée*

2 teaspoons icing/confectioners' sugar

280 g/10 oz. white chocolate, chopped

100 g/7 tablespoons butter

piping bag, fitted with a plain nozzle/tip

baking sheets, lined with non-stick parchment paper

MAKES ABOUT 25

To make the raspberry ganache, start the day before you want to bake the macarons. Put the raspberry purée and sugar in a saucepan and gently bring to simmering point. Add the chocolate and butter and stir until melted. Remove from the heat and whisk with an electric whisk until smooth. Cover and refrigerate for 24 hours.

The next day, preheat the oven to 145°C (275°F) Gas 1. Bring the ganache to room temperature.

Make the Vanilla Macaron Shells as described on page 60 but just after you have piped them onto the baking sheets, sprinkle a tiny amount of the crystallized rose petals on top of each round – not too much otherwise the macarons won't rise. Rest and bake as normal.

Fill the piping bag with the ganache and pipe some onto the flat underside of half of the cold macarons. Add a lychee quarter and sandwich with another macaron shell.

*To make your own raspberry purée, put 360 g/3 cups raspberries and 40 g/3½ tablespoons caster/superfine sugar in a food processor or blender and blitz until smooth. Strain through a sieve/strainer before using.

RASPBERRY CHEESECAKE MACARONS

Who can resist cheesecake? Imagine it sandwiched inside a very pretty macaron and you've got a true Franco-American hybrid sweet. This is the perfect guilty treat when you crave a sugar hit after a hard day!

1 quantity Vanilla Macaron Shells (page 60, but follow the method here)

pink food colouring

about 13 raspberries, halved, to fill

CHEESECAKE FILLING

½ vanilla bean

75 g/⅓ cup cream cheese

75 ml/⅓ cup double/heavy cream

75 ml/⅓ cup single/light cream

100 g/3½ oz. sweetened condensed milk

1 egg

small, round silicone mould

piping bag, fitted with a plain nozzle/tip

baking sheets, lined with non-stick parchment paper

small pastry or paint brush

MAKES ABOUT 25

To make the cheesecake filling, preheat the oven to 110°C (225°F) Gas ¼.

Split the vanilla bean lengthways and scrape the seeds out into a mixing bowl with the remaining cheesecake ingredients. Beat with an electric whisk until well combined. Transfer the mixture to the small, round mould and bake in the preheated oven for about 20 minutes. Allow to cool completely in the mould and raise the oven temperature to 145°C (275°F) Gas 1.

Make and bake the Vanilla Macaron Shells as described on page 60. Allow to cool on the baking sheets. When cold, dip a small pastry or paint brush into the pink food colouring and very gently paint swirls onto each macaron shell.

Scoop the cooked cheesecake into the piping bag. Pipe some onto the flat underside of half of the cold macarons. Add a halved raspberry and sandwich with another macaron shell.

MOJITO MACARONS

Let's get the party started! It's time to make a cheeky macaron for a fun party and what better idea is there than a cocktail-inspired bite? A little taste of Havana with rum, lime and fresh mint, these macarons have a pleasant mojito sourness that will surprise your guests! Consume without moderation…

1 quantity Vanilla Macaron Shells (page 60, but follow the method here)

grated zest of 1 lime

green food colouring

RUM GANACHE

100 ml/⅓ cup plus 1 tablespoon single/light cream

50 g/2 oz. mascarpone

300 g/10½ oz. white chocolate, chopped

2 teaspoons butter

2 tablespoons white rum

5 fresh mint leaves, finely chopped

piping bag, fitted with a plain nozzleltip

baking sheets, lined with non-stick parchment paper

MAKES ABOUT 25

To make the rum ganache, start the day before you want to bake the macarons. Put the cream and mascarpone in a saucepan, mix and gently bring to the boil. Add the chocolate and butter and stir until melted. Add the rum and mint, remove from the heat and blitz in a food processor until smooth. Transfer to a bowl, cover and refrigerate for 24 hours.

The next day, preheat the oven to 145°C (275°F) Gas 1. Bring the ganache to room temperature.

Make the Vanilla Macaron Shells as described on page 60, adding the lime zest to the food processor with the ground almonds. Tint the mixture your preferred shade of green by very gently mixing in some green food colouring. Don't mix it in completely – you want to leave splodges of colouring in the mixture to create a dappled effect on the macaron shells later. Pipe, rest and bake as normal.

Fill the piping bag with the ganache and pipe some onto the flat underside of half of the cold macarons. Sandwich with another macaron shell.

CARROT-TOP MACARONS

This is a very brave recipe hiding a truly unusual soul: carrot, cumin and orange. They complement each other beautifully and result in such a striking macaron with a uniquely exotic taste.

1 quantity Vanilla Macaron Shells (page 60, but follow the method here)

grated zest of ½ orange

orange food colouring

CUMIN GANACHE

100 ml/⅓ cup plus 1 tablespoon single/light cream

50 g/2 oz. mascarpone

300 g/10½ oz. white chocolate, chopped

1 teaspoon butter

1–2 pinches ground cumin

CANDIED CARROTS

2 carrots, peeled and cut into ultra-thin slices

50 ml/3½ tablespoons orange juice

100 g/½ cup (caster) sugar

piping bag, fitted with a plain nozzle/tip

baking sheets, lined with non-stick parchment paper

MAKES ABOUT 25

To make the cumin ganache, start the day before you want to bake the macarons. Put the cream and mascarpone in a saucepan and gently bring to the boil. Add the chocolate and butter and stir until melted. Add the cumin, remove from the heat and whisk with an electric whisk until smooth. Cover and refrigerate for 24 hours.

The next day, bring the ganache to room temperature.

To make the candied carrots, put 100 ml/⅓ cup and the remaining ingredients in a saucepan over medium heat and cook for about 15 minutes or until the sugar has dissolved and the carrots are tender. Allow to cool while you make the macarons.

Preheat the oven to 145°C (275°F) Gas 1.

Make the Vanilla Macaron Shells as described on page 60, adding the orange zest to the food processor with the ground almonds. Tint the mixture your preferred shade of orange by very gently mixing in some orange food colouring. Pipe oblong shapes on the prepared baking sheets. Space the shapes about 3 cm/1¼ inches apart. Rest and bake as normal.

Drain and dry the slices of candied carrot. Fill the piping bag with the ganache and pipe some onto the flat underside of half of the cold macarons. Add a slice of candied carrot and sandwich with another macaron shell.

TEA VOYAGE MACARONS

A bite of these macarons will transport you to the other end of the world and fill you with zen-like contentment. The green tea and jasmine extract make this a perfect option for a tea party.

finely chopped pistachios, to sprinkle

TEA GANACHE

100 ml/⅓ cup plus 1 tablespoon single/light cream

50 g/2 oz. mascarpone

300 g/10½ oz. white chocolate, chopped

1 teaspoon butter

1 teaspoon matcha (green tea) powder

2 drops of pure jasmine extract

VANILLA MACARON SHELLS

240 g/1¾ cups icing/confectioners' sugar

140 g/1½ cups ground almonds

½ vanilla bean

5 egg whites

50 g/¼ cup caster/superfine sugar

piping bag, fitted with a plain nozzle/tip

baking sheets, lined with non-stick parchment paper

MAKES ABOUT 25

To make the tea ganache, start the day before you want to bake the macarons. Put the cream and mascarpone in a saucepan and gently bring to the boil. Add the chocolate and butter and stir until melted. Remove from the heat and whisk with an electric whisk until smooth. Stir in the matcha powder and jasmine extract. Cover and refrigerate for 24 hours.

The next day, preheat the oven to 145°C (275°F) Gas 1. Bring the ganache to room temperature.

To make the vanilla macaron shells, sift the icing/confectioners' sugar into a food processor, add the almonds and blitz thoroughly. Split the vanilla bean lengthways and scrape the seeds out into a grease-free mixing bowl. Add the egg whites and whisk with an electric whisk until stiff peaks form. Gradually add the caster/superfine sugar, whisking until all the sugar is used up and the egg whites are glossy.

Fold the blitzed sugar/almonds into the egg whites until well combined and smooth. Fill the piping bag with the mixture and pipe neat 4-cm/1½-inch rounds on the prepared baking sheets. Space the rounds 3 cm/1¼ inches apart. Sprinkle a tiny amount of finely chopped pistachios on top of each round – not too much otherwise the macarons won't rise.

Allow to set for 30–60 minutes until a skin forms – you should be able to touch the surface of the macarons very gently with a wet finger without sticking to them.

Bake in the preheated oven for about 12 minutes. Allow to cool on the baking sheet.

Fill the piping bag with the ganache and pipe some onto the flat underside of half of the cold macarons. Sandwich with another macaron shell.

AFTER-DINNER MACARONS

The combination of sweet, rich chocolate and fresh mint is a classic, and in this macaron, it makes a perfect after-dinner treat. The crystallized mint leaves are a nice ice-cold surprise when you bite into the traditional chocolate macaron shells.

crystallized mint leaves, to fill

CHOCOLATE GANACHE

165 ml/¾ cup single/light cream

135 g/5 oz. dark/bittersweet chocolate (55% cocoa), chopped

2 teaspoons butter

CHOCOLATE MACARON SHELLS

220 g/1½ cups icing/confectioners' sugar

130 g/1⅓ cups ground almonds

25 g/¼ cup cocoa powder

5 egg whites

50 g/¼ cup caster/superfine sugar

piping bag, fitted with a plain nozzle/tip

baking sheets, lined with non-stick parchment paper

MAKES ABOUT 25

To make the chocolate ganache filling, start the day before you want to bake the macarons. Pour the cream into a saucepan and gently bring to the boil. Add the chocolate and butter and stir until melted. Remove from the heat and whisk with an electric whisk until smooth. Cover and refrigerate for 24 hours.

The next day, preheat the oven to 145°C (275°F) Gas 1. Bring the ganache to room temperature.

To make the chocolate macaron shells, sift the icing/confectioners' sugar into a food processor, add the ground almonds and blitz until thoroughly mixed. Sift in the cocoa powder and blitz again. Put the egg whites into a grease-free mixing bowl and whisk with an electric whisk until stiff peaks form. Gradually add the caster/superfine sugar, whisking until all the sugar is used up and the egg whites are glossy.

Fold the blitzed sugar/almonds into the egg whites until well combined and smooth. Fill the piping bag with the mixture and pipe neat 4-cm/1½-inch rounds on the prepared baking sheets. Space the rounds 3 cm/1¼ inches apart.

Allow to set for 30–60 minutes until a skin forms – you should be able to touch the surface of the macarons very gently with a wet finger without sticking to them.

Bake in the preheated oven for about 12 minutes. Allow to cool on the baking sheet.

Fill the piping bag with the ganache and pipe some onto the flat underside of half of the cold macarons. Add a crystallized mint leaf and sandwich with another macaron shell.

INDEX